LaDainian Tomlinson

Jim Gigliotti
AR B.L.: 5.5 Alt.: 853
Points: 1.0   MG

LaDainian TOMLINSON

By Jim Gigliotti

The Child's World®

www.childsworld.com

Published in the United States of America by The Child's World®
1980 Lookout Drive • Mankato, MN 56003-1705
800-599-READ • www.childsworld.com

ACKNOWLEDGMENTS

The Child's World®: Mary Berendes, Publishing Director

Produced by Shoreline Publishing Group LLC
President / Editorial Director: James Buckley, Jr.
Designer: Tom Carling, carlingdesign.com

Photo Credits: Cover: Joe Robbins.
Interior: Getty Images: 1, 14, 16, 19, 21, 24, 25, 27;
Joe Robbins: 3, 5, 7, 8, 11, 23, 28

LIBRARY OF CONGRESS
CATALOGING-IN-PUBLICATION DATA

Gigliotti, Jim.
  Ladainian Tomlinson / by Jim Gigliotti.
    p. cm. — (The world's greatest athletes)
  Includes index.
  ISBN 978-1-59296-881-7 (library bound : alk. paper)
 1. Tomlinson, LaDainian. 2. Football players—United States—
Biography—Juvenile literature. I. Title. II. Series.

GV939.T65.G54 2008
796.332092—dc22
 [B]

                                    2007031996

CONTENTS

A New Scoring King Is Crowned

SAN DIEGO CHARGERS RUNNING BACK LADAINIAN "LT" Tomlinson waits for the snap of the ball. His hands rest on his knees while his eyes look over the field. The Chargers have the football at the Cincinnati Bengals' nine-yard line.

The ball is hiked to the quarterback, and LaDainian starts to his left. He takes a **pitchout** from Philip Rivers, his quarterback. LaDainian catches the ball and takes several more big steps to his left. His head is up and his eyes, always alert, spot a hole in the defense. Suddenly, he plants his left foot solidly on the ground, and he cuts back to the right.

Quick as a cat, LT is through the opening. A defender lunges, but grabs nothing but air. LT's at the ten. He's at the five. He's in the end zone. Touchdown!

This is the type of play that has been repeated again and again during LaDainian's career in the National Football League (NFL). When the Chargers score a touchdown, it's usually Number 21 with the ball. It happened so often in 2006, in fact, that LaDainian set an NFL record for touchdowns in a season. He reached the end zone a remarkable 31 times.

LaDainian Tomlinson combines speed, vision, and talent like few others.

How does he do it? Well, like many great running backs, LaDainian has excellent speed. Like some, too, he is tough and durable. Like others, he is an excellent receiver, giving his quarterback another way to move the ball. And he has instincts that help him choose just which part of the defense to attack and when.

But the thing about LT is that he combines all of those **attributes** in one complete package. It is what sets him apart from any other running back in the NFL today . . . and maybe ever.

CHAPTER 1

Best Running Back Ever?

YOU MIGHT HAVE HEARD YOUR PARENTS OR YOUR grandparents talk about watching Michael Jordan play basketball. "He was the greatest that ever was," they might say. "You should have seen him."

Or maybe it was Willie Mays in baseball that they marveled at. Or Wayne Gretzky in hockey. Well, guess what? When you grow older, you'll be able to tell your kids and your grandkids that you got to see LaDainian Tomlinson when he was at his best. "He was the best that ever was," you might say. "You should have seen him."

Until now, most people felt that the greatest running back ever to play in the NFL was Jim Brown or Walter Payton. Brown was a star for the Cleveland Browns in the late 1950s and early 1960s. He was at

In just a few seasons, LT has placed himself among the greatest runners of all time—and he's just getting better!

the height of his career when he retired following the 1965 season. Payton was such a gifted runner on the field and a pleasant man off it that he was nicknamed "Sweetness." Payton played for the Chicago Bears from 1975 to 1987. He was a big reason that LaDainian, who was eight years old when Payton retired, wanted to grow up to be a football player.

Walter Payton was the NFL's all-time leading runner until his career total was topped by Emmitt Smith in 2004.

"I've wanted to play football ever since I was six years old and saw Walter Payton play," LaDainian said when he appeared on TV's "The Tonight Show" during the 2006 season. "He was the reason I wanted to be a running back."

In the 1990s, Barry Sanders and Emmitt Smith were two more running backs who have sometimes been called the best ever. Sanders electrified NFL fans with his amazing moves for the Detroit Lions. He ran for more than 1,000 yards in each of his 10 seasons. Smith played most of his career with the Dallas Cowboys. He retired in 2004 with an all-time record 18,355 rushing yards in his career.

But the talk about "the greatest ever" all changed when LaDainian set his NFL record in 2006. Instead of just considering him a really good player by today's standards, experts began considering LT one of the best of all time.

Marty Schottenheimer, who was LaDainian's head coach in San Diego from 2002 to 2006, often has called Tomlinson the best running back that he has seen in his 40 years in football. But late in the 2006 season, the veteran head coach Schottenheimer took it a step further.

In His Own Words

You won't hear LaDainian Tomlinson call himself the best running back ever. He is much too humble for that. (In fact, when NFL Network once asked him to rate the top backs of all time, he put Walter Payton at the top of the list.) But you can be sure that is exactly what he is trying to become. To get there, he knows he has to put in the hours in the offseason—when the cameras aren't on and the fans aren't around. This is how he put it, when asked by *The Sporting News*:

"It's all about whether you have it to be the best. You can talk about it, but will you truly put in the time when no one is watching? How do you want to be remembered? Do you want to be a legend in the game or someone just playing for the money? I feel I am a very talented player, but how much better would I be if I do these workouts? No one knows—but why not try to be the greatest? I could [tell myself] how good I am. Or I could be doing something about it. If I am not doing something, someone else is getting the edge on me, to be better than me, and I just refuse to let anyone be better than me."

"I believe he is the finest running back ever to wear a uniform," he said. "That's how I feel."

Sometimes, coaches, fans, or the **media** overstate a player's skills when he has a great season. LT is no one-year wonder, though. LaDainian has had one great season after another ever since he first came into the league in 2001. It's just that more people started taking notice.

From pregame stretching to offseason workouts, LT knows that he has to combine hard work with his talent to succeed.

After receiving little attention in high school, LT was a breakout success in college wearing the purple uniform of TCU.

CHAPTER 2

Foundation for Success

FOR A LITTLE WHILE, LADAINIAN HAD TROUBLE getting anyone to take notice. Such as college football **recruiters**, for instance.

That's because LT didn't always get to carry the football at University High School in Waco, Texas. In fact, in his first season with the varsity (when he was a sophomore in 1994), LaDainian played linebacker. The next year, he moved to offense but he was a fullback. Finally, as a senior in 1996, he became the starting tailback.

Looking back, maybe that's how LaDainian got to be such a well-rounded player. He had to be tough to be a linebacker. He had to block well to be a fullback. And only after that did he get to showcase his skills as a runner.

And what a runner he was! In the first game of his senior season, LaDainian scored five touchdowns. By the end of the year, he had rushed for 2,554 yards. He scored 39 touchdowns in 15 games. However, only a few local colleges offered him scholarships.

LaDainian decided to attend Texas Christian University (TCU), which had had some great players in its history, but which had not been very good for a long time. And the Horned Frogs (yes, that's the school's nickname!) weren't good in LT's first year there, either: They won only one game. But in each of the next three years, in large part because of LaDainian, TCU won more games than it lost.

In LT's senior season in 2000, he was a finalist for the Heisman Trophy, the award given each year to the best college football player. His fourth-place finish was a big accomplishment considering that he wasn't playing at a powerhouse school.

His biggest game came against Texas-El Paso in 1999. The magic number for a running back is 100 yards. LT reached that—and much more! With 406 yards in that game, which TCU won 45-25, he became the only player in NCAA Division I-A history to top 400 rushing yards in a game.

Young LaDainian Tomlinson

▶ Was born in Rosebud, Texas, and grew up in nearby Waco, where he became a big Dallas Cowboys' fan.

▶ Played lots of different sports growing up. But he loved his current sport so much that he slept with a football beside him each night.

▶ Was 13 years old when he attended the Emmitt Smith Football Camp at the University of North Texas. He remembers taking a handoff from the former Cowboys' star, who is now the NFL's all-time leading rusher.

▶ Did not become the starting tailback until his senior season at University High School in Waco. In his first game that year, he scored 5 touchdowns.

▶ Met his wife, Torsha, while the two were students at Texas Christian University.

In his senior year, LaDainian ran for 2,158 yards. It was the most in the nation for the second year in a row. He finished his college career with 5,263 rushing yards. That was the sixth most in NCAA Division I-A history. The young man who had started out as a linebacker was ready now to take the next step—to the NFL.

CHAPTER 3

An Instant NFL Star

At the NFL Draft, NFL Commissioner Paul Tagliabue welcomed
LT to the Chargers . . . and life as a pro football player.

AS THE 2001 **NFL DRAFT** APPROACHED, THE Chargers were scheduled to have the number-one choice. That's because they had the poorest record in the league the previous season (teams choose in reverse order of the standings). But San Diego decided to trade that pick and wound up choosing fifth instead—and the Chargers still ended up with the best player in the draft. Here's how it happened.

Going into the draft, almost everyone agreed that the player to pick number one was quarterback Michael Vick. He was a great runner as well as a passer, and the kind of player who only rarely comes around. Almost everyone agreed that San Diego needed a quarterback, too. It seemed to be a perfect fit.

The trouble was, San Diego needed lots of things. The Chargers had a miserable season in 2000 in which they won only once in 16 games. They not only needed a quarterback, but they also needed a running back, a wide receiver, some offensive linemen, linebackers . . . well, you get the idea.

So the **front office** decided to trade the number-one pick to the Atlanta Falcons. In return, San Diego got Atlanta's first-round pick, which was the fifth choice overall, plus another player and future picks.

A lot of media and fans were shocked that the Chargers would pass up a chance to take Vick. But it turned out to be a brilliant move. The Chargers got several players with the Falcons' picks who helped them for many years, plus they still got a good quarterback when they drafted Drew Brees with their own choice in the second round. The big trade eventually turned the Chargers into winners again.

"I'd say both teams **prospered** quite well in the trade," Chargers coach Marty Schottenheimer said three years later, when Vick and Tomlinson both led their teams to the playoffs.

The most important player in the equation for San Diego, of course, was LaDainian. He wasted no time making an impact. In his very first game, he ran for 113 yards and scored two touchdowns. More importantly, the Chargers stunned Washington 30-3. The next week, LT ran for 90 yards and San Diego beat the Cowboys 32-21 to double its win total from '01. Then it was 107 yards and three touchdowns in a 28-14 victory over the Bengals.

The Chargers were the surprise team of the NFL, and Tomlinson was a hero in San Diego. Though the team cooled off after that, LT did not. He finished the

Score one for the rookie! LT celebrates after scoring one of the three touchdowns he gained against Cincinnati in 2001.

season with 1,236 rushing yards. It was the most by a rookie in club history.

LT followed up his fabulous rookie season by rushing for 1,683 yards and scoring 15 touchdowns in 2002. He made the **Pro Bowl** for the first time that year. (He's done it three times since). In 2003 he ran for 1,645 yards, scored 17 touchdowns, and caught an amazing 100 passes. No other player in NFL history has run for at least 1,000 yards and caught 100 passes in the same season.

In 2004, he began a streak of 18 consecutive games with a touchdown. That tied an NFL record set by Lenny Moore way back in 1965. In 2005, in a game against the Raiders, LT ran for a touchdown, caught a touchdown pass, and passed for a touchdown—only six other players in NFL history ever have done all three in a single game!

On top of all that, the Chargers got even more than just an incredible football player. They got one of football's top citizens, too. "He is Superman without the cape," says Chargers fullback Lorenzo Neal.

LaDainian's charity group is called the Tomlinson Touching Lives Foundation. The foundation hosts football camps and golf tournaments, and buys holiday gifts for children in the hospital and awards scholarships to good students.

At every home game, too, LaDainian hosts 21 (his uniform number) kids from youth groups in the San Diego area. He doesn't just give them tickets, either. He takes pictures with them and lets them come down on the field after the game.

By the end of the 2004 season, LT was the Chargers' all-time leader in rushing.

Man of the Year

LaDainian Tomlinson has won many, many awards during his football career. (This book probably isn't even big enough to talk about all of them!) The one he is most proud of, however, is the Walter Payton NFL Man of the Year Award, which he shared with New Orleans Saints quarterback Drew Brees for 2006.

LT cherishes the award because it recognizes players for their contributions to the community, as well as for their play on the field. Plus, it's named in honor of his boyhood idol.

"I wanted to be like Walter Payton when I was growing up," LaDainian said. "He was more than a great running back. He was a great person. Torsha [LT's wife] and I have been blessed, and we're grateful to be able to continue his leadership that had such a positive impact on kids just like me growing up."

It also was fitting that LaDainian shared the award with his good friend Brees. They first met a high school all-star game in Texas and were teammates on the Chargers from 2001 to 2005.

CHAPTER 4

LT's Record– Breaking Season

EVERYTHING THAT LADAINIAN HAD DONE IN HIS marvelous pro career was just a hint of what was to come in 2006. That's when everything came together during a once-in-a-lifetime season.

LT opened the year by rushing for 131 yards and scoring a touchdown in a 27-0 **rout** of division-rival Oakland. That was a nice start, but it hardly gave any hint of what was to come because the Raiders were clearly overmatched. So were the Titans, against whom LaDainian scored two touchdowns the next week in a lopsided, 40-7 win.

Six games into the season, LaDainian still had only that one 100-yard game against the Raiders. Would you believe some people in the media and in the stands were wondering if he was slowing down?

Defenders, like these Cleveland Browns, tried everything to stop LT in 2006, but nothing kept him from setting records.

LaDainian's Big Moment

With a little over three minutes left in a game against Denver late in 2006, the Chargers recovered a fumble at the Broncos' seven-yard line. It was no secret who would get the ball next. Everyone on the field, on the sidelines, and in the stands knew that LT had tied the NFL record of 28 touchdowns in a season only a few moments earlierd. Now all that was left was for LT to break the record.

On a play called "Power 50," LaDainian took a handoff from Philip Rivers. The play was designed to go inside, but LT's instincts told him to take it outside instead. With a quick fake, he beat a Broncos' cornerback and stepped just inside the left corner to score the record touchdown. He was lifted onto his teammates' shoulders as the Chargers' fans chanted, "LT! LT! LT!"

It was an incredible accomplishment for LaDainian. Typically, however, he took greater joy in what San Diego's 48-20 win meant for the team. "It is extra meaningful," he said after the game. "Not only did I get the record, but we clinched a playoff spot, and we won the division. So many things happened today that were special for this football team."

But LT knew what was going on. The Chargers were breaking in a new quarterback—Philip Rivers. He was a first-round draft choice in 2004 who spent three seasons learning behind former starter Drew Brees. When Brees became a **free agent** and signed with New Orleans in 2006, Rivers stepped in.

Until Rivers proved that he could give the Chargers a passing attack, other teams were going to concentrate on stopping LT as much as possible. "Now defenses are going to have to stay honest," LaDainian predicted after Rivers had a good passing

In 2006, the improvement of quarterback Philip Rivers (17) helped open up new holes for LT to run through.

day against San Francisco. "As the season goes on, I'm looking to have some big games on the ground."

LT's words turned out to be **prophetic**. In a 38-24 victory over St. Louis in the seventh game of the year, he ran for 187 yards and scored three touchdowns. Then he scored three more touchdowns against Cleveland. And then four against Cincinnati. In one of the most remarkable streaks in NFL history, LaDainian scored 28 touchdowns in a 10-week stretch that started in that game against the 49ers. No other player ever scored more times in an entire 14- or 16-game season!

When LaDainian scored his third touchdown in a victory over Denver in week 14, he broke Shaun Alexander's NFL record of 28 touchdowns. After he had finally broken the record, LT sounded more relieved than anything else. "The ride is still going," he said. "But the hoopla is over about the record. As much as you try to avoid it, you think about it and people talk about it. So as a player, you just want to get it over with—if it's going to happen—as fast as possible. Now I can go back to just playing football."

LaDainian eventually earned NFL most valuable player honors for 2006. His final totals were

After almost all of his touchdowns, LT doesn't do big dances or spike the ball . . . he just flips it away and gets back to work.

staggering: 1,815 rushing yards, 56 receptions, 2,323 yards from scrimmage (that's rushing yards plus receiving yards), and 31 touchdowns. He was every opposing NFL coach's nightmare.

So how do you follow up the kind of a season that most athletes couldn't approach even in their wildest imagination? Well, the answer to that one is easy. Even with all of LT's individual accomplishments, the year ended on a sour note when the Chargers, who had the best record in the NFL with 14 wins and only two losses during the regular season, lost their first playoff game (to New England). That means a Super Bowl championship, not more records, remains LaDainian's ultimate goal.

For now, he'll have to be content with knowing that he had one of the best seasons of any football player in history.

"When we're old and can't play this game anymore," he told the media shortly after breaking the touchdown record, "these are the moments we are going to remember. This is what we'll be able to tell our kids, and tell our grandchildren." Who knows, maybe one day you'll tell your kids the same thing—that you saw the best ever.

Looking ahead, LT has one more big goal: a Super Bowl championship.

LaDainian Tomlinson's Career Statistics

BORN: June 23, 1979   **BIRTHPLACE:** Rosebud, Texas

HEIGHT: 5-10   **WEIGHT:** 221

COLLEGE: Texas Christian University   **DRAFTED:** 2001 (first round)

Year	Team	RUSHING No.	Yards	Avg	TD	RECEIVING No.	Yards	Avg	TD
2001	Chargers	339	1236	3.6	10	59	367	6.2	0
2002	Chargers	372	1683	4.5	14	79	489	6.2	1
2003	Chargers	313	1645	5.3	13	100	725	7.3	4
2004	Chargers	339	1335	3.9	17	53	441	8.3	1
2005	Chargers	339	1462	4.3	18	51	370	7.3	2
2006	Chargers	348	1815	5.2	28	56	508	9.1	3
Career	Chargers	2050	9176	4.5	100	398	2900	7.3	11

GLOSSARY

attributes   qualities that make a person good at what he or she does

free agent   a player who has finished his contract with one team and is allowed to sign with any other team

front office   nickname for the people who are in charge of making decisions about players on an NFL team

media   the television, radio, and Internet reporters who cover a team and tell the public about it

NFL draft   the process by which pro teams pick college players

pitchout   a short backward toss, usually made underhanded and usually from a quarterback to a running back

Pro Bowl   the NFL's annual all-star game

prophetic   to correctly tell about an event ahead of time

prospered   did well

recruiters   members of a college coaching staff who try to convince a player to come to their school to play sports

rout   a defeat by a large margin

BOOKS

1001 Facts About Running Backs
By Brian Peterson
New York: DK Publishing, 2003.
This pocket-sized book is filled with interesting trivia and facts about great NFL running backs past and present—including, of course, LaDainian Tomlinson.

The History of the San Diego Chargers
By Adam Schmalzbauer
Mankato, Minnesota: Creative Education, 2005.
Read the story of LT's team from its beginning in 1960 to the exciting days of the 2000s.

LaDainian Tomlinson: All-Pro On and Off the Field
By Craig Ellenport
Berkeley Heights, New Jersey: Enslow Publishers, 2006.
This biography is part of the "Sports Stars With Heart" series. It not only talks about LaDainian's remarkable accomplishments on the field, but also how he uses his star status to help others who are less fortunate than he is.

WEB SITES

Visit our Web page for lots of links about LaDainian Tomlinson and the NFL: www.childsworld.com/links

Note to Parents, Teachers, and Librarians: We routinely check our Web links to make sure they're safe, active sites—so encourage your readers to check them out!

INDEX

ABOUT THE AUTHOR

Jim Gigliotti is a writer who lives in southern California with his wife and two children. A former editor with the National Football League's publishing division, he has written more than a dozen books about sports and personalities, including *Stadium Stories: USC Trojans* and *Watching Football* (with former NFL star Daryl Johnston).